Algrove Publishing Limited
1090 Morrison Drive
Ottawa, Ontario
Canada K2H 1C2

Canadian Cataloguing in Publication Data

Strong, Chas. J. (Charles Jay), b. 1865
    Strong's book of designs

(Classic reprint series)
Reprint of ed. published: Chicago : F.J. Drake & Co., 1917.
ISBN 1-894572-24-6

    1. Decoration and ornament. I. Strong, L. S. (Lawrence
Stewart), b. 1888. II. Title. III. Series: Classic reprint series (Ottawa, Ont.)

TT360.S87 2001   745.4   C00-901607-4

Printed in Canada
#20901

STRONG'S BOOK OF DESIGNS

A Masterpiece of Modern Ornamental Art

COMPRISING NEW IDEAS AND DESIGNS OF EVERY
CONCEIVABLE SORT OF INTEREST TO THE SIGN
PAINTER, CARD WRITER AND COMMERCIAL ARTIST

INCLUDING

Air Brush Designs, Posters, Show Cards, Business Cards,
Letter Heads, Sign Ends, Ribbons, Scrolls, Panels, Book
Covers, Hanging Signs, also Thirty Pages of Ornamental
Work in Color, and Numerous Alphabets

By CHAS. J. STRONG and L. S. STRONG
of the Detroit School of Lettering

NEW AND ENLARGED EDITION

FREDERICK J. DRAKE & COMPANY
Publishers, CHICAGO

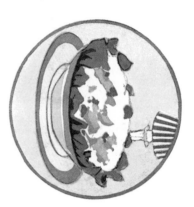

BOOK OF DESIGNS

BY

C J Strong

BULLETIN

Script

STOCKING FILLERS

EASTER

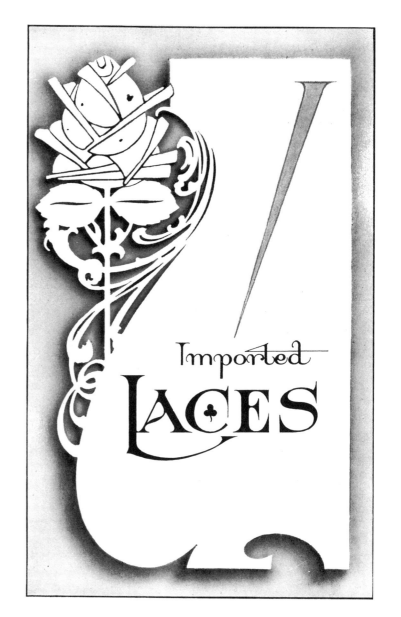

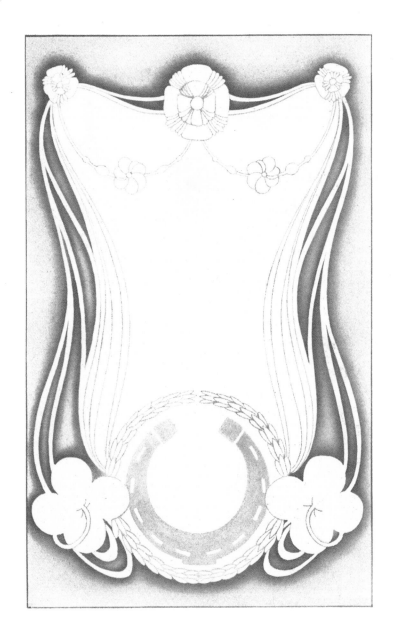

THE COSY THEATRE

HOLIDAY BILL

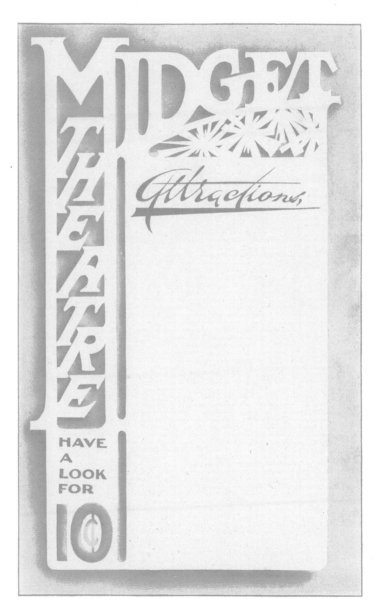

MIDGET THEATRE

Attractions

HAVE A LOOK FOR 10

CASINO
5¢

Program

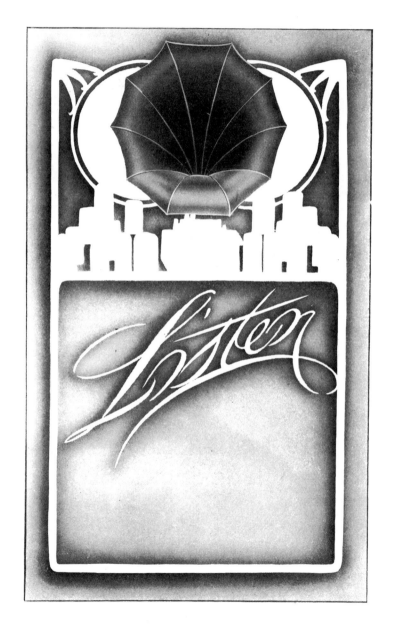

Listen

MODERN STYLES LETTER DECORATION

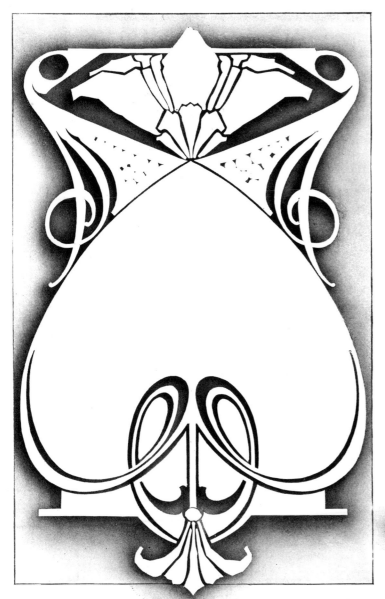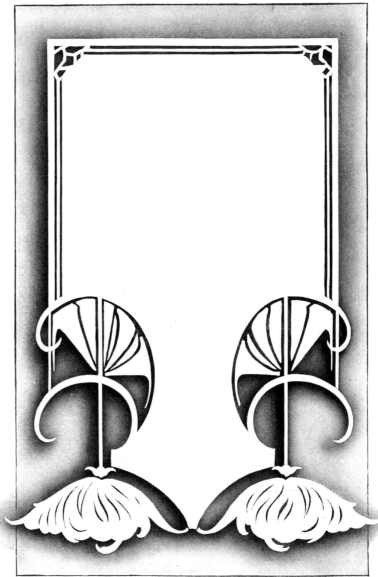

EMPIRE THEATRE

THE ROYAL

TO DAYS FEATURES

Thanks-

-giving..

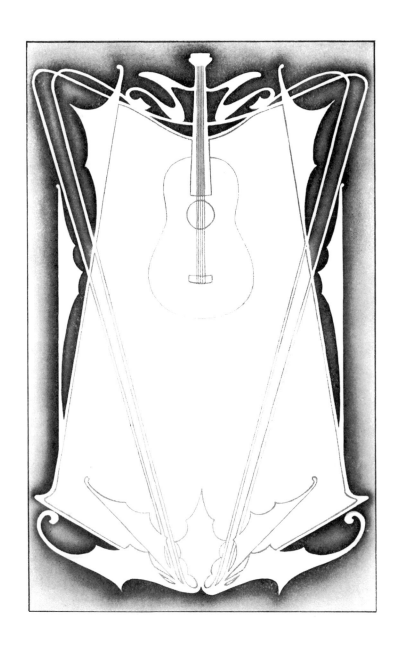

PRACTICAL
SCROLLS

ALREADY
FOR THE BIG
MOONLITE XCURSION
TO SO & SO
SOME THURSDAY

SMITH WILL SIGN ANYTHING

CALL ME UP

121 Blank St

BIGTOWN N. Y.

Smith will SIGN anything

121 BLANK ST. BIGTOWN, N.Y.

CALL HIM UP

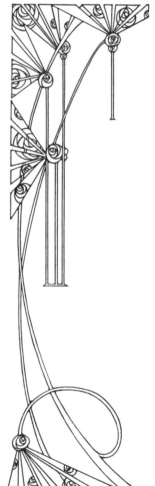

Business Cards

SMITH & SMITH
SIGN
PAINTERS

PHONE
2002

MAIN
FLOOR

121 BLANK ST. BIGTOWN N.Y.

SMITH & SMITH

PHONE
2002

MAIN
FLOOR

SIGNS

121 BLANK ST. BIGTOWN N.Y.

HAVE
A CARD.

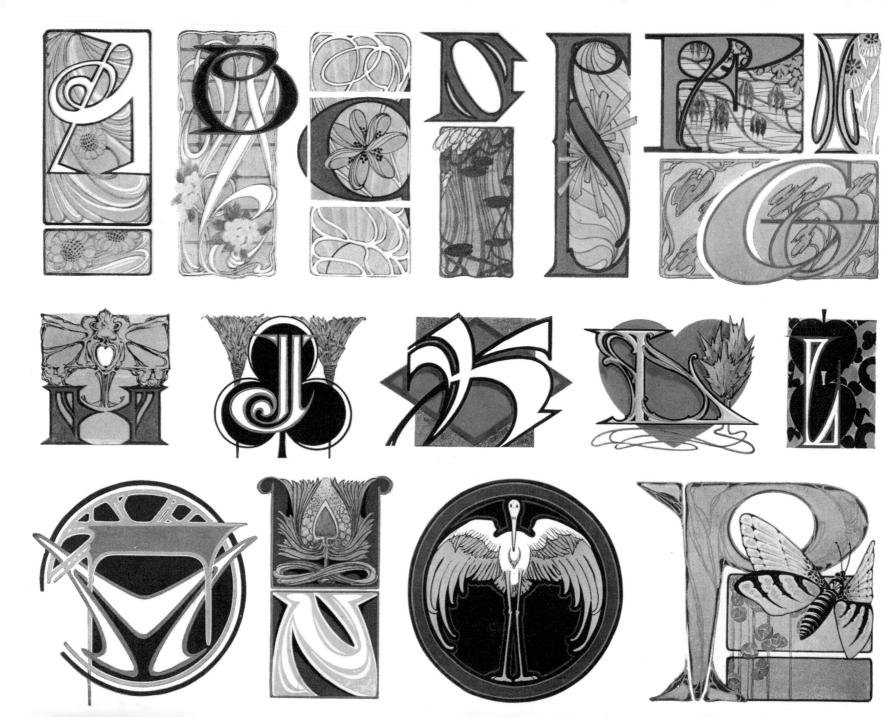

WOLVERINE

Automobile Company

Detroit · · · Michigan

HIGH GRADE AUTOMOBILES

Wolverine
Automobiles

General Purpose
Touring Cars and
Runabouts

Monroe Colliery Co.

FAIRMONT GAS COAL

EUREKA SHARPENER COMPANY

MANUFACTURERS OF
LAWN MOWER
SHARPENERS

S. O. Marrausa PRINTING CO.

50-52-54 TENTH ST.

I WILL
SIGN
ANYTHING

Call me up

Smith

121 BLANK ST.

BIGTOWN, N.Y.

I WILL
SIGN
ANYTHING

Call
me
up.

Smith

121 BLANK ST   BIGTOWN, N.Y.

Card

suggest/ions.

Peculiar Decoration.

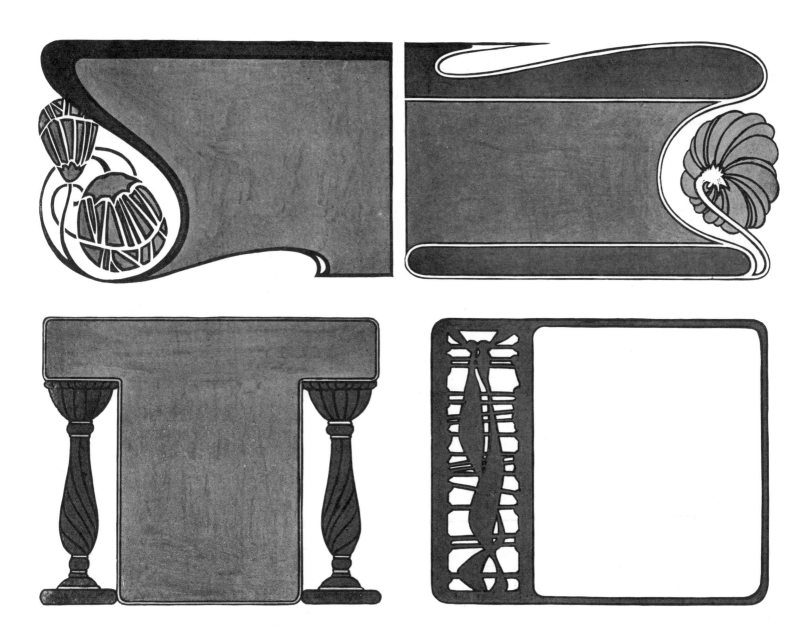

Odds
and
Ends

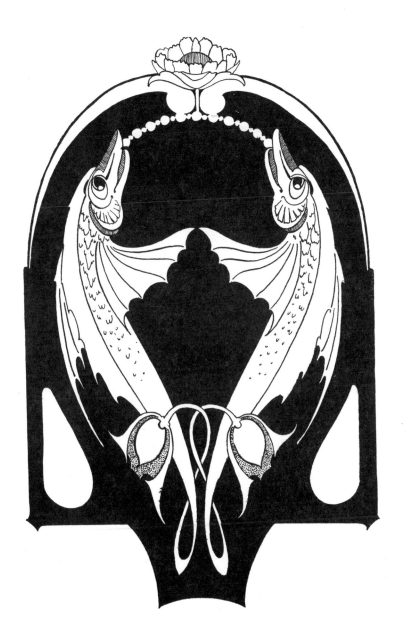

HANDY IDEAS

SIGNS

We make 'em — while you wait.

SHOW CARDS

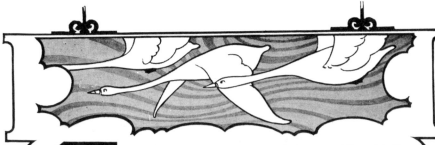

GAME

·IN SEASON·

SELECTED

FURS

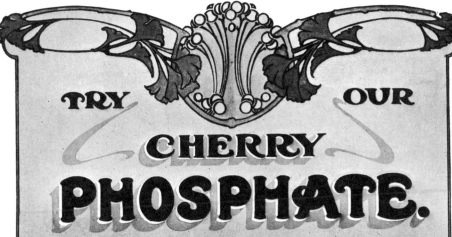

TRY OUR

CHERRY

PHOSPHATE.

52

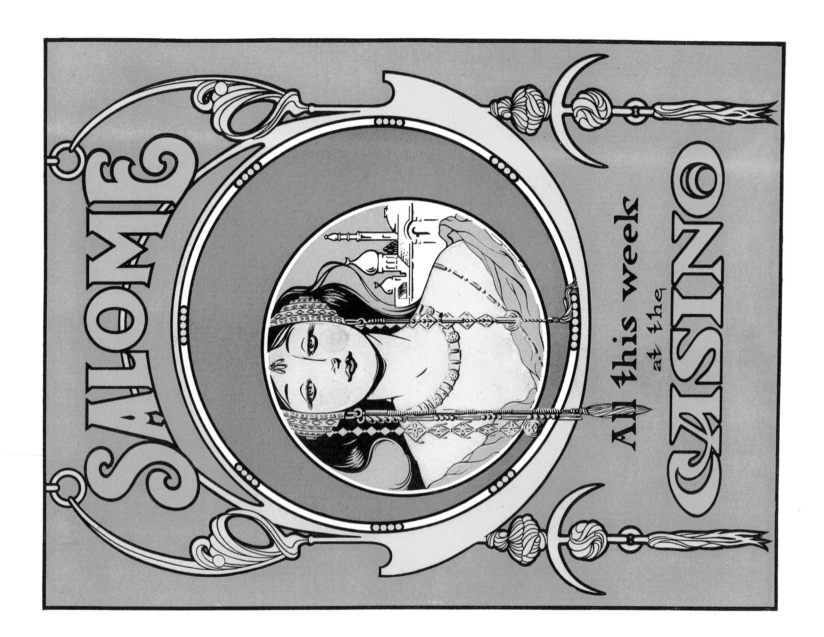

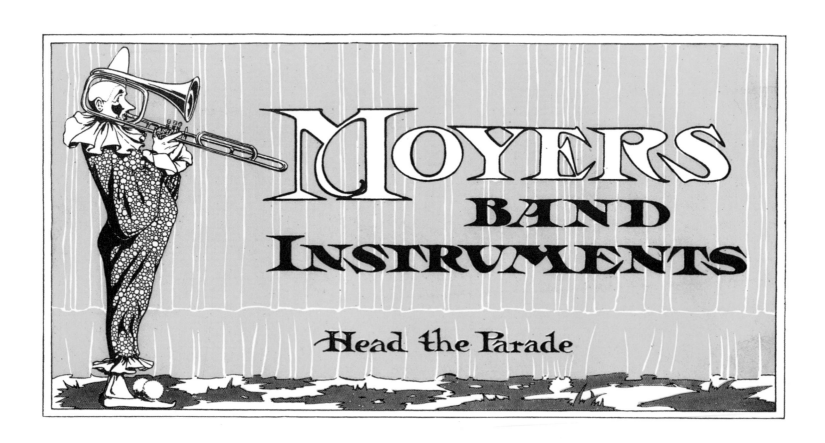

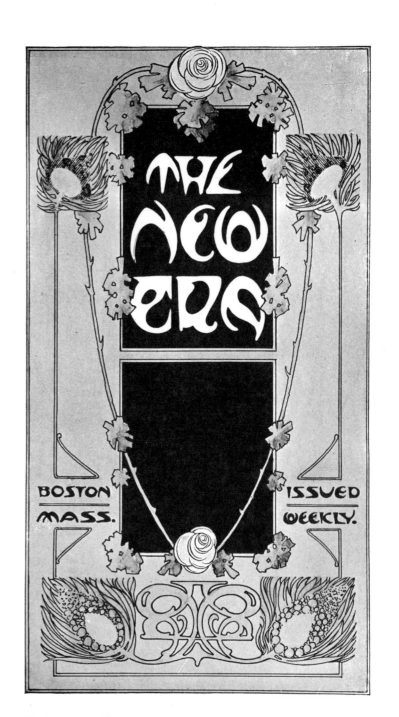

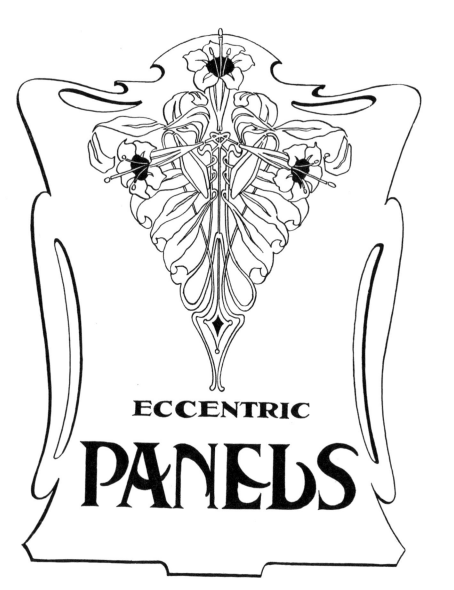

ECCENTRIC
PANELS

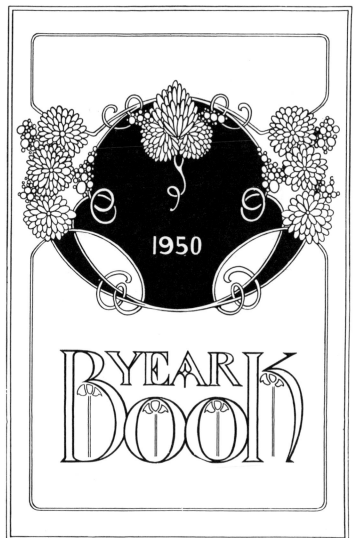

1950

YEAR
BOOK

RIBBONS

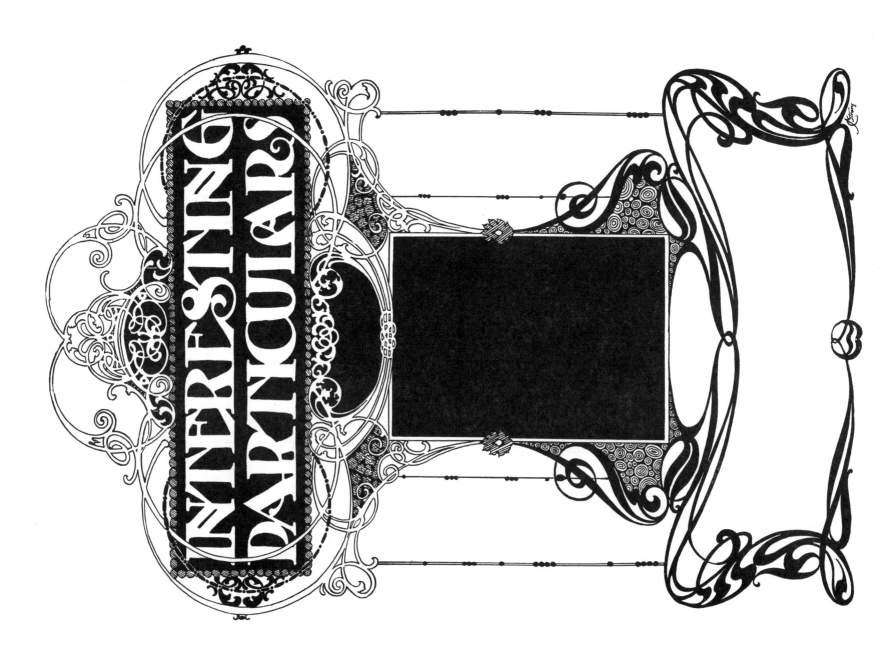

INTERESTING PARTICULARS

Tablet Design.

DRUGS

Things Vncommon

Unloading SALE

**Everything Must Go
Nothing Reserved**

ALL
PRICES
CUT
IN
HALF

SHE AND ME

A TALE OF WE?? TIMES.

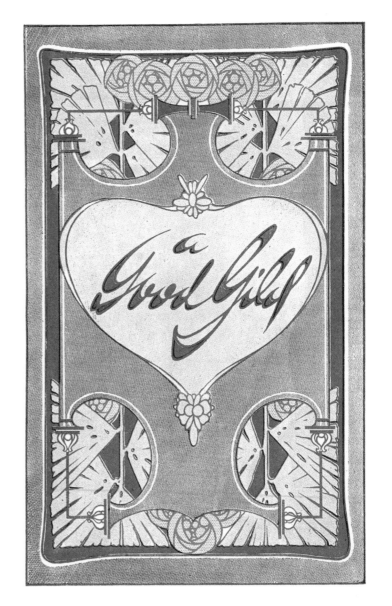

A Good Gild

A GOOD HORSE THOROUGHLY BROKE IS VALUABLE **BUT** A GOOD MAN THOROUGHLY BROKE ISN'T WORTH A CENT

BUY HERE AND SAVE MONEY.

A customer that gets the "BUTT-END" of a deal goes straight up and **NEVER COMES BACK!**

WE HAVE NO "STRONG BUTTER"

Daily
BARGAIN
BULLETIN.

MENS *Fleece* **SUITS**
Lined
Riveted
Buttons
Warm &
Cool.

Marked down
from $10. to

10¢

A **FACT**
that
sounds like a
JEST.

All wool
double-
story

COLLARS

1¢ *each*

SLEEPY

OR LIFE OF A BOY IN A SIGN SHOP

BY
I. Ben There.

THE
GOOD
OLD
SUM-
MER
TIME

BY S. PLUNK.

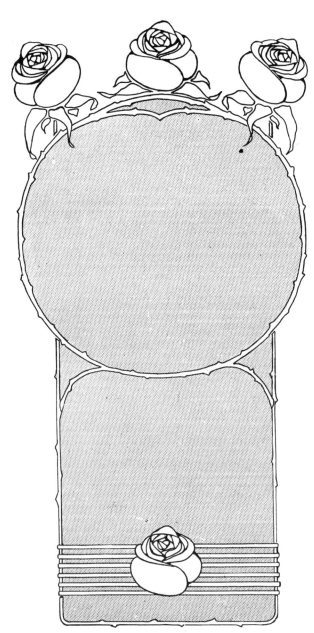

Fine FLOWERS MAKE Fine HATS

Pen and ink work

CASE

PLOW

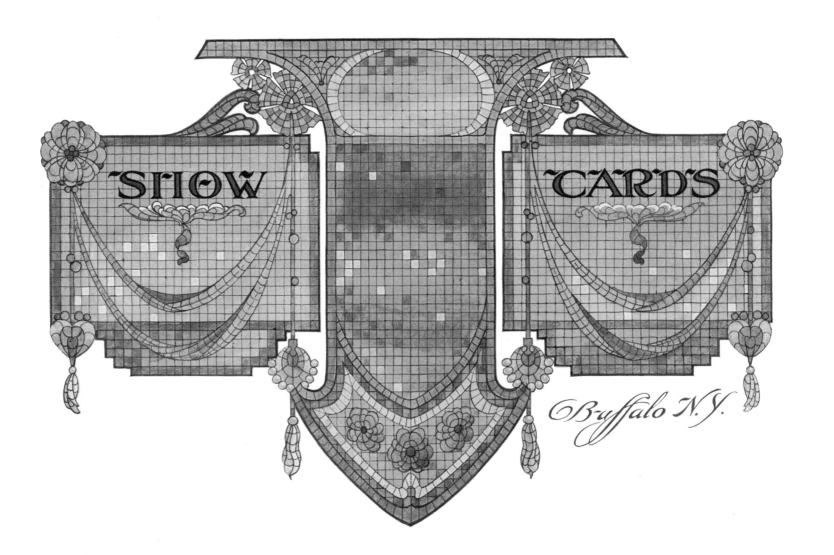

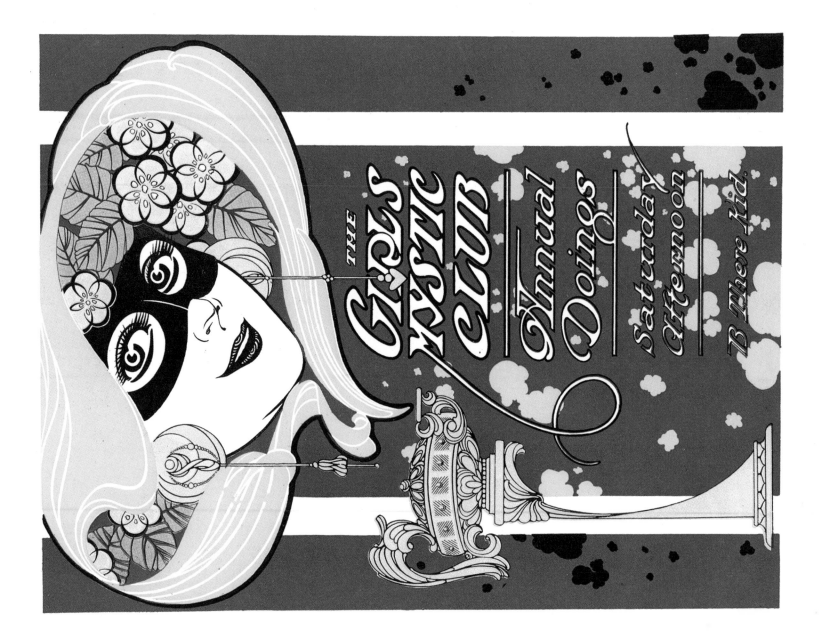

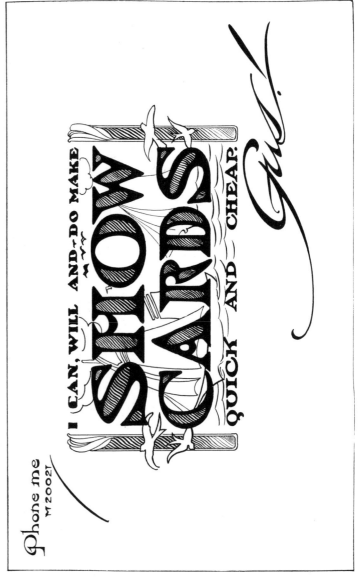

SKATING at Belle Isle

Good Music 5

There & Back Ten Cents.

BULLETIN & DESIGNS

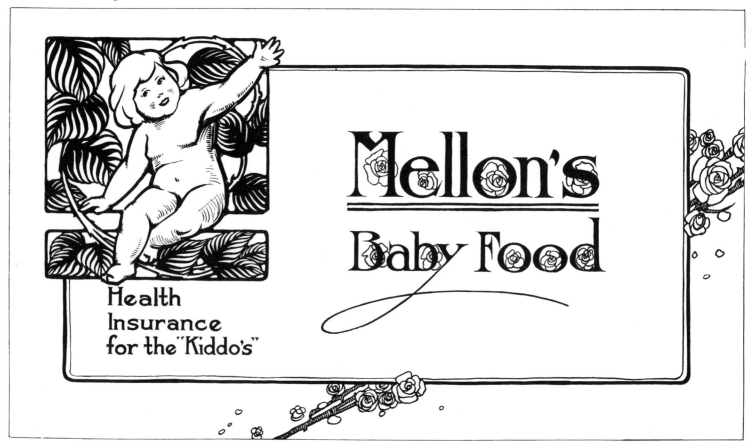

Health
Insurance
for the "Kiddo's"

Mellon's
Baby Food

CARD ❦ IDEAS

Dull-Season
SALE
BUNKS

186 BROADWAY.

Come early
Come quick
Choice goods 1/2 off

BULLETIN DESIGN

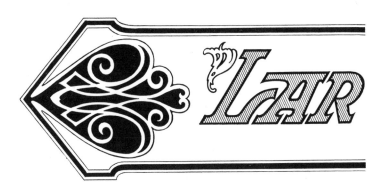

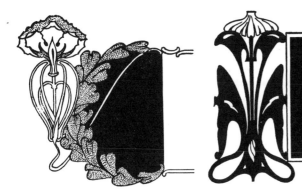
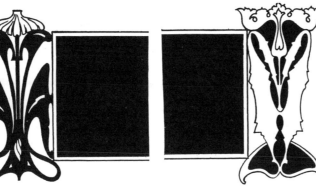
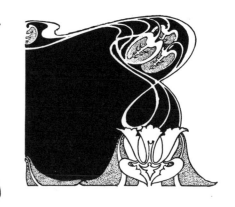

ESTATE

CO.

210
AND
212
BOYS
SUITS

ABCD
EFGHIJKL
MNOPRST
UVWXYZ

ABC

DEFGHI

JKLMNOPQ

RSTUV

WXYZ

ABCD

EFGHIJKL

MNOPRST

UVWXYZ

ABC
DEFGHIJ
KLMNOP
RSTUV
WXYZ

ABGD

ḂƑGHIJ̣KL

MNOPRST

UVWXYZ

ABCDEFG
HIJKLMN
OPRSTUV
WXYZ
123456789

ABCD

EFGHIJKL

MNOPRST

UVWXYZ

ABCD

EFGHIJKL

MNOPRST

UVWXYZ

ABCDEF

GHIJKLMN

OPPRSST

UVOXYE

abcdefghhijklmnn

opqrstfauvwxyzz